I Love My Body

A 30-day affirmation guide
to a healthy, beautiful body.

by LOUISE L. HAY

HAY HOUSE
Santa Monica, CA
HAY HOUSE

Hay House, Inc.
Santa Monica, CA
(213) 828-3666

First printing March, 1985
Fourth printing November, 1987
Manufactured in the United States of America

ISBN 0-937611-02-6

9 8 7 6 5

To all the bodies on the planet,
I dedicate this offering with love.

30 Days to a Healthy Body

Little babies love every inch of their bodies (including their own feces). They have no guilt, no shame, and no comparison. You were like that, and then somewhere along the line you listened to others who told you you were "not good enough." You began to criticize your body thinking that perhaps that's where your flaws were.

Let's drop all that nonsense and get back to loving our bodies and accepting them totally as they are. Of course they will change—and if we give our bodies love, they will change for the better.

The subconscious mind has no sense of humor and does not know false from true. It only accepts what we say and what we think as the material from which it builds. By repeating these "I LOVE MY BODY" affirmations over and over, we will be planting new seeds in the fertile soil of your subconscious mind, and they will become true for you.

Stand in front of a mirror and repeat each affirmation and the new thought patterns ten times. Do this twice a day. Also write the affirmations ten times sometime during the day. Work with one affirmation a day until you have gone through the whole booklet. Then if there is any part of your body you still dislike or have a problem with—use that particular affirmation daily for at least a month, or until positive change takes place.

If doubts or fears or negative thoughts come up, just recognize them for what they are—old limiting beliefs that want to stay around. They have no power over you. Say to them gently, "Out! I no longer need you." Then repeat your affirmation again.

In this way, within a short time you will have a body you really love. And your body will respond by giving you excellent health. Each part of your body will be working perfectly as a harmonious whole. You will even find lines disappearing, weight normalizing, and posture straightening.

That which we constantly affirm must become true for us.

Notes

Day 1

I Love My Mind

My Mind enables me to recognize the beautiful Miracle of my Body. I am glad to be alive. I affirm with my Mind that I have the power to heal myself. My Mind chooses the thoughts that create my future moment by moment. My power comes through the use of my Mind. I choose thoughts that make me feel good. I love and appreciate my beautiful Mind!

Notes

Day 2

I Love My Hair

I trust the process of life to take care of my every need and I grow strong and peaceful. I relax my scalp and give my beautiful hair room to grow luxuriously. I lovingly groom my hair and choose the thoughts that support its growth and strength. I love and appreciate my beautiful hair!

Notes

Day 3

I Love My Eyes

I have perfect vision. I see clearly in every direction. I see with love my past, my present and my future. My mind chooses the way I look at life. I see with new eyes. I see the good in everyone and everywhere. I now lovingly create the life I love to look at. I love and appreciate my beautiful eyes!

Notes

Day 4

I Love My Ears

I am balanced and poised and one with all of life. I choose the thoughts that create harmony around me. I listen with love to the good and the pleasant. I hear the cry for love that is hidden in everyone's message. I am willing to understand others, and I have compassion for them. I rejoice in my ability to hear life. I have a receptive capacity of mind. I am willing to hear. I love and appreciate my beautiful ears!

Notes

Day 5

I Love My Nose

I am at peace with everyone around me. No person, place or thing has any power over me. I am the power and authority in my world. I choose the thoughts that recognize my own true worth. I recognize my own intuitive ability. I trust my intuition for I am always in contact with Universal Wisdom and Truth. I always go in the right direction for me. I love and appreciate my beautiful nose!

Notes

Day 6

I Love My Mouth

I nourish myself by taking in new ideas. I prepare new concepts for digestion and assimilation. I make decisions with ease based upon the principles of Truth. I have a good taste for life. I choose the thoughts that enable me to speak with love. I speak up for myself secure in my own true worth. I love and appreciate my beautiful mouth!

Notes

Day 7

I Love My Neck

I willingly turn to acknowledge other viewpoints and other ways of doing things. I am free to acknowledge it all. I am willing to change. I choose the thoughts that keep me flexible in my ideas and in my creative expression. I express myself freely and joyously. I am safe. I love and appreciate my beautiful neck!

Notes

Day 8

I Love My Shoulders

I shoulder my responsibilities with ease. My burdens are light—like feathers in the wind. I stand tall and free and I joyfully carry my experiences. My shoulders are beautiful and straight and strong. I choose the thoughts that make my way easy and free. Love releases and relaxes. I love my life. I love and appreciate my beautiful shoulders!

Notes

Day 9

I Love My Arms

I am protective of myself and of my loved ones. I welcome life with joy. I have great ability to embrace life's experiences. My capacity for the enjoyment of life is enormous. I choose the thoughts that enable me to accept change easily and move in any direction. I am strong and able and capable at all times. I love and appreciate my beautiful arms!

Notes

Day 10

I Love My Hands

My hands are free to hold life in any way they wish. My hands have endless ways of handling events and people. I choose the thoughts that handle my experiences with joy and with ease. Each detail is taken care of in Divine right order. I handle life with love; therefore, I am secure, I am safe, I am myself. I am at peace. I love and appreciate my beautiful hands!

Notes

Day 11

I Love My Back

I am supported by life itself. I feel emotionally supported. I release all fears. I feel loved. I release the past and all past experiences. I let go of that which is in back of me. I now trust the process of life. I choose the thoughts that supply all my needs. Life prospers me in expected and unexpected ways. I know that life is for me. I stand straight and tall supported by the love of life. I love and appreciate my beautiful back!

Notes

Day 12

I Love My Chest

I take in and give out nourishment in perfect balance. Life supplies everything I need. I am free to be me, and I allow others the freedom to be who they are. Life protects us all. It is safe for all of us to grow up. I nourish only with love. I choose the thoughts that create freedom for us all. I love and appreciate my beautiful chest!

Notes

Day 13

I Love My Lungs

I have a right to take up space. I have a right to exist. I take in and give out life fully and freely. It is safe to take in my environment. I trust the Power that supplies my breath in such great abundance. There is enough breath to last for as long as I shall choose to live. There is enough life and sustenance to last for as long as I shall choose to live. I now choose the thoughts that create safety for me. I love and appreciate my beautiful lungs!

Notes

Day 14

I Love My Glands

My glands are the starting points for my Self-expression. My Self-expression is my own unique approach to life. I am a unique individual. I respect my individuality. I originate in the depth of my being all the good I find unfolding in my life. My originality begins with the thoughts I choose to think. My spiritual immunity and strength are strong and balanced. I am a go-getter. I have "get up and go." I love and appreciate all my beautiful glands!

Notes

Day 15

I Love My Heart

My heart lovingly carries joy throughout my body, nourishing the cells. Joyous new ideas are now circulating freely within me. I am the joy of life expressing and receiving. I now choose the thoughts that create an ever-joyous now. It is safe to be alive at every age. I radiate love in every direction, and my whole life is a joy. I love with my heart. I love and appreciate my beautiful heart!

Notes

Day 16

I Love My Stomach

It is with joy that I digest the experiences of life. Life agrees with me. I easily assimilate each new moment of every day. All is well in my world. I choose the thoughts that glorify my being. I trust life to feed me that which I need. I know my self-worth. I am good enough just as I am. I am a Divine, Magnificent Expression of Life. I assimilate this thought and make it true for me. I love and appreciate my beautiful stomach!

Notes

Day 17

I Love My Liver

I let go of everything I no longer need. I joyfully release all irritation, criticism and condemnation. My consciousness is now cleansed and healed. Everything in my life is in Divine right order. Everything that happens is for my highest good and greatest joy. I find love everywhere in my life. I choose the thoughts that heal, cleanse and uplift me. I love and appreciate my beautiful liver!

Notes

Day 18

I Love My Kidneys

It is safe for me to grow up and to accept the life I have created. I release the old and welcome the new. My kidneys efficiently eliminate the old poisons of my mind. I now choose the thoughts that create my world; therefore, I accept everything in my world as perfect. My emotions are stabilized in love. I love and appreciate my beautiful kidneys!

Notes

Day 19

I Love My Spleen

My only obsession is with the joy of life. My true identity is one of peace and love and joy. I choose the thoughts that create joy for me in every area of my life. My spleen is healthy and happy and normal. I am safe. I choose to experience the sweetness of life. I love and appreciate my beautiful spleen!

Notes

Day 20

I Love My Waistline

I have a beautiful waistline. It is normal and natural and very flexible. I can bend and twist in every direction. I choose the thoughts that allow me to enjoy exercise in a form that is pleasing to me. My waistline is the perfect size for me. I love and appreciate my beautiful waistline!

Notes

Day 21

I Love My Hips

I carry myself through life in perfect balance. There is always something new I am moving toward. Every age has its interests and goals. I choose the thoughts that keep my hips firm and powerful. I am powerful at the very seat of my life. I love and appreciate my beautiful hips!

Notes

Day 22

I Love My Colon

I am an open channel for good to flow in and through me—freely, generously and joyfully. I willingly release all thoughts and things that clutter or clog. All is normal, harmonious and perfect in my life. I live only in the ever-present now. I choose the thoughts that keep me open and receptive to the flow of life. I have perfect intake, assimilation and elimination. I love and appreciate my beautiful colon!

Notes

Day 23

I Love My Bladder

I am at peace with my thoughts and emotions. I am at peace with those around me. No person, place or thing has any power over me, for I am the only thinker in my mind. I choose the thoughts that keep me serene. I willingly and lovingly release old concepts and ideas. They flow out of me easily and joyously. I love and appreciate my beautiful bladder!

Notes

Day 24

I Love My Genitals

I rejoice in my sexuality. It is normal and natural and perfect for me. My genitals are beautiful and normal and natural and perfect for me. I am good enough and beautiful enough exactly as I am, right here and right now. I appreciate the pleasure my body gives me. It is safe for me to enjoy my body. I choose the thoughts that allow me to love and approve of myself at all times. I love and appreciate my beautiful genitals!

Notes

Day 25

I Love My Rectum

I see the beauty of my body in every cell and in every organ. My rectum is as normal and natural and beautiful as any other part of my body. I am totally accepting of each function of my body and rejoice in its efficiency and perfection. My heart and my rectum and my eyes and my toes are all equally important and beautiful.
I choose the thoughts that allow me to accept with love every part of my body. I love and appreciate my beautiful rectum!

Notes

I Love My Legs

I now choose to release all old childhood hurts and pains. I refuse to live in the past. I am a now person living in today. As I forgive and release the past, my thighs become firm and beautiful. I have total mobility to move in any direction. I move forward in life unencumbered by the past. My calf muscles are relaxed and strong. I choose the thoughts that allow me to move forward with joy. I love and appreciate my beautiful legs!

Notes

Day 27

I Love My Knees

I am flexible and flowing. I am giving and forgiving. I bend and flow with ease. I have understanding and compassion, and I easily forgive the past and everyone in it. I acknowledge others and praise them at every turn. I choose the thoughts that keep me open and receptive to the love and joy that is flowing freely everywhere. I kneel at the altar of myself. I love and appreciate my beautiful knees!

Notes

Day 28

I Love My Feet

I have such wonderful understanding. I stand firmly rooted in the Truth. My understanding of myself and of others and of life itself is constantly growing. I am nourished by Mother Earth, and the Universal Intelligence teaches me all I need to know. I walk upon this planet safe and secure moving forward toward my greater good. I move with ease through time and space. I choose the thoughts that create a wonderful future, and I move into it. I love and appreciate my beautiful feet!

Notes

Day 29

I Love My Skin

My individuality is safe. The past is forgiven and forgotten. I am free and safe in this moment. I choose the thoughts that create joy and peace for myself. My skin is youthful and smooth on every part of my body. I love to caress my skin. My cells have eternal youth. My skin is the mantle that protects the temple I live in. I love and appreciate my beautiful skin!

Notes

Day 30

I Love My Body

My body is a glorious place to live. I rejoice that I have chosen this particular body because it is perfect for me in this lifetime. It is the perfect size and shape and color. It serves me so well. I marvel at the miracle that is my body. I choose the healing thoughts that create and maintain my healthy body and make me feel good. I love and appreciate my beautiful body!

Notes

Notes

Notes

Notes

Holistic Healing Recommendations

BODY

Nutrition

Diet, Food Combining, Macro-Biotic, Natural Herbs, Vitamins, Bach Flower Remedies, Homeopathy.

Exercise

Yoga, Trampoline, Walking, Dance, Cycling, Tai-Chi, Martial Arts, Swimming, Sports, Etc.

Alternative Therapies

Acupuncture, Acupressure, Colon Therapy, Reflexology, Radionics, Chromotherapy,
Massage & Body Work
- Alexander, Bioenergenics, Touch for Health, Feldenkrais, Deep Tissue Work, Rolfing, Polarity, Trager, Reiki.

Relaxation Techniques

Systematic Desensitization, Deep Breathing, Biofeedback, Sauna, Water Therapy (Hot Tub), Slant Board, Music.

Books

Getting Well Again - Simonton
Herbally Yours - Royal
How to Get Well - Airola
Food Is Your Best Medicine - Bieler
You Can Heal Your Body - Hay

MIND

Affirmations, Mental Imagery, Guided Imagery, Meditation, Loving the Self.

Psychologial Techniques

Gestalt, Hypnosis, NLP, Focusing, T.A., Rebirthing, Dream Work, Psycho Drama, Past Life Regression, Jung, Humanistic Psychotherapies, Astrology, Art Therapy.

Groups

Insight, est, Loving Relationship Training, ARAS, Ken Keyes Groups, All 12-Step Programs, Aids Project, Rebirthing.

Books

Creative Visualization - Gawain
Visualization - Bry
Focusing - Gendlin
The Power of Affirmations - Frankhauser
Superbeings - Price
Love is Letting Go of Fear - Jampolsky
Teach Only Love - Jampolsky
A Conscious Person's Guide to Relationships - Keyes
Moneylove - Gillies
Loving Relationships - Ray
Celebration of Breath - Ray
You Can Heal Your Life - Hay

SPIRIT

Prayer

Asking for What You Want, Forgiveness,
Receiving (Allowing the Presence of God to Enter),
Accepting, Surrendering.

Spiritual Group Work

M.S.I.A., T.M., Siddah Foundation,
Rajneesh Foundation, Self Realization,
Religious Science, Unity

Books

Course in Miracles - Foundation for Inner Peace
Autobiography of a Yogi - Yogananda
Any book by Emmett Fox
The Nature of Personal Realty - Roberts
Your Needs Met - Addington
The Manifestation Process - Price
The Science of Mind - Holmes

Louise L. Hay, whose first book, "Heal Your Body," was published in 1976, is an internationally known leader in the New Age Movement. Her list in that book of more than 200 mental causes for physical illness and her affirmations for overcoming them are quoted far and wide by other healers, seminar leaders, body workers, rebirthers, other ministers and metaphysicians.

Louise's second book, "You Can Heal Your Life," came on the market in December of 1984. She feels it will surpass even the wide popularity of "Heal Your Body."

As a metaphysical counselor, Louise devotes her life to assisting others in discovering and using the full potential of their own innate healing powers. Her students are able to clear away the blocks that keep them from robust health and from having what they want in life.

A frequent guest on radio and television, Louise is a minister and teacher of Science of Mind. She makes her home in Santa Monica, California.